Your 60 Minute Lean Business

Standardised Work

Your 60 Minute Lean Business
Standardised Work
October 2012
First Edition

www.lulu.com
ISBN: 978-1-300-30015-1
Copyright © 2012 Jason Tisbury

All rights reserved. No part of this publication may be reproduced or transmitted in any form or by any means, electronic or mechanical, including photocopying, recording, or by any information storage and retrieval system, without the written permission of the author, except where permitted by law.

Also by Jason Tisbury:

Your 60 Minute Lean Business:
5S Implementation Guide
Total Productive Maintenance

7 Steps To A Lean Business

Contents

Title	Page
Foreword	5
What is Standardised Work?	7
Benefits of Standardised Work	9
Takt Time	11
The Three Slips and Kaizen	13
Slip 1 - Production Capacity Sheet	18
Slip 2 - Standardised Work Combination Table	26
Slip 3 - Standardised Work Chart	43
Other Documents	47
Quality Standards	52
Analysis and Kaizen	54
Next Steps	56

Foreword

Welcome to the Lean Business in 60 Minutes series of books. Why 60 minutes? Well for a couple of reasons. It occurred to me a number of years ago while searching through libraries and book stores for texts on the topic of lean manufacturing and lean business that most of the available books were quite large and often not easy to understand for someone new to the topic. The essence of lean is to remove waste from a business and its processes, yet here were all of these books that were filled with non-essential words – waste. I felt a book on the topic of lean should itself be lean. With this in mind I went about writing my first book on lean – 7 Steps To A Lean Business – an overview of lean manufacturing and lean business systems. At 140 pages, this book can be read in a couple of hours and while the details may not enable one to immediately turn a business lean, I believe 7 Steps does provide a very sound overview and ground learning for the lean newcomer.

Now it is time to share the details of some of the different lean tools, I started writing a book detailing all of the tools but soon realised what I was writing wasn't lean enough. And so the Lean Business in 60 Minutes idea was conceived. Starting with 5S and TPM, the series is now working through the Lean House.

If you are a business owner or manager and are looking for a concise, detailed guide to understanding standardised work, then this book was written especially for you. My goal is to share what I have been lucky enough to learn with other like minded people who may not have had the dumb luck that I have had. When I say dumb luck, I mean dumb luck. The following is the story of how I came to learn lean, I'm sharing this story to firstly build my credentials and secondly to show how anybody can learn and implement these tools.

At the age of 32 I was working in a factory after a recent business failure when I was lucky enough to break two fingers in a ten ton press. It was quite a bad break, twelve months recovery including two surgeries (one bone graft). Now it may seem strange to call that lucky, but luck is what you make of a situation. Even though I had only one working hand, I could still use a computer, and I was fairly handy on a computer (pun not intended). I ended up working with the Quality Manager who by chance was starting to implement some lean manufacturing / continuous improvement ideas in the business. I learnt a great deal during this time. I was also lucky that this company was in the automotive industry and that one of their main customers was Toyota, probably the best company in the world to learn from. I spent the next five years living and breathing the Toyota Production System (TPS) with direct instruction and mentoring through Toyota. Now after having implemented lean systems and tools through a variety of companies in many organisations in many diverse industries, it is time to share what I have learnt for others to benefit.

What is Standardised Work?

Standardised work is probably one of the most commonly known elements of the lean system. Lean gets its basis from the Toyota Production System (TPS); behind kanban, standardised work is one of the better known tools of TPS and is one of the base elements (as can be seen in the below diagram).

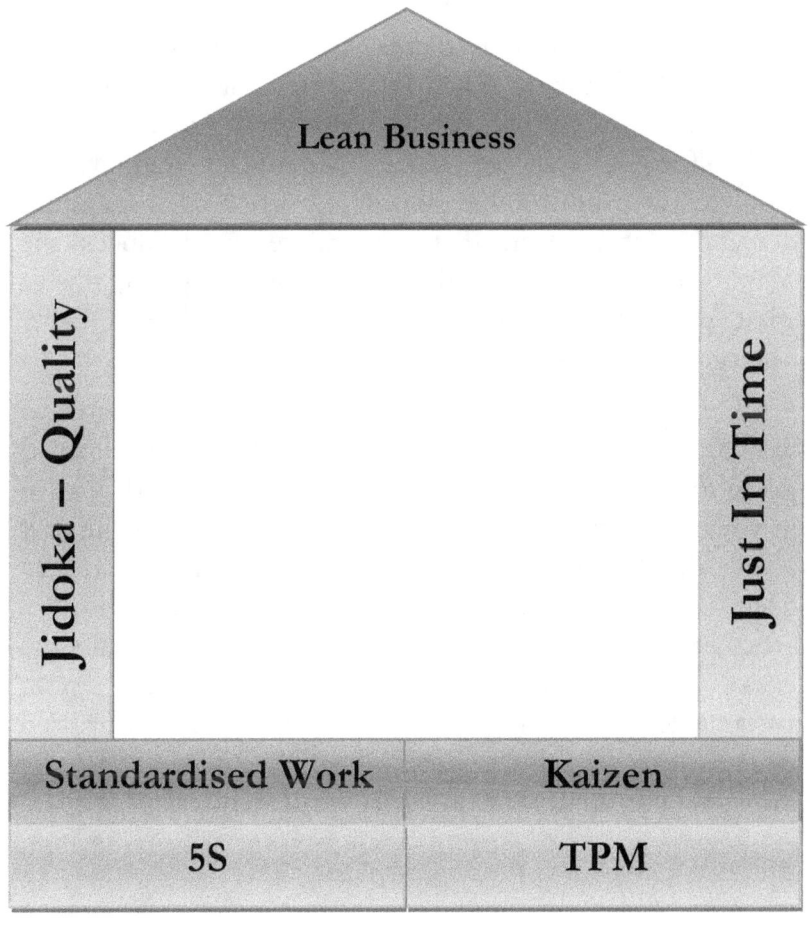

There is a common misconception that the goal of standardised work is to turn the workforce into robots and make everyone do the same thing everyday. While it is true we need a consistent process to give us consistent and expected outputs, the use of the word 'robot' is far too strong. In fact, the major factor in the success of Toyota over the years has been its 'respect for the people' philosophy. This will be explained later in the chapter "Standardised Work and Kaizen".

So what exactly is standardised work? Put simply, it is system of breaking down the work to its elements and reassembling these elements to develop a process that is both efficient and effective. Efficient in that it will consistently produce the outputs to satisfy the customer demand. Effective in that it consistently produces the outputs to the quality and specifications required, this is what we call a process that is 'in control' in Quality Management speak.

This is a very simplistic explanation of standardised work, in the coming pages you will find a far more detailed guide to implementing your own standardised work system in your business. It is important to understand though, that standardised work is just one tool in the lean system. By itself, standardised work will provide some benefits, both to efficiency and quality; when used in conjunction with the entire lean toolkit, you business will become more sustainable in every aspect. So don't stop with standardised work, unlock your businesses true potential by implementing an holistic and effective lean business system.

Benefits of Standardised Work

Expanding on the above explanation, the available benefits of standardised work include:

- Consistent process control
- Improved quality
- Improved efficiency
- Reduced costs
    - Operating
    - Capital
- Early detection of problems
- Improved customer satisfaction

Because standardised work enables consistency, lower management (frontline managers) can spend more time solving important problems and working on new improvements rather than 'putting out fires'. This creates a more positive work environment that actually self perpetuates further efficiency gains.

Further to all of this standardised work actually creates a culture of employee engagement in improving processes. By following a standard process, it becomes easy to gauge the effect of new approaches; process change becomes more scientific. Changes to the process can be tested and measured against very stable baseline data, this makes proving the benefit or otherwise of these changes clear and unarguable. This encourages all staff (especially those working on the process) to identify improvement opportunities.

With a standardised process, auditing becomes much easier. Deviations from the process become obvious (even for senior management) when implemented correctly. This brings us to Genchi Genbutsu; the Gemba is Japanese meaning "the real place" or the place where value is created. Genchi Genbutsu is another Japanese term meaning to "go see"; see the problem at the source. In manufacturing the source is the manufacturing floor. When standardised work is implemented properly, it will be easy for every level of management to observe the work and conduct an audit against the standardised work. This enables the management to be actively involved in problem solving with the operators. This is dependent on the standardised work being clearly documented; without this documentation the management team would require an in-depth knowledge of the processes to enable similar problem solving capability.

Standardised work is not only useful in manufacturing though, it can be just as effective in warehousing, distribution, office and healthcare. In fact most organisations that have effectively implemented standardised work have found that it is only truly effective when it has been implemented across the entire organisation.

TAKT Time

Takt translates from German as 'cycle time', however in lean manufacturing it refers to the rate of customer demand. Takt time plays an integral role in standardised work as the customer demand requirement becomes our target cycle time and gives us something to measure our performance against.

Calculating the takt time can be performed by using the following formula:

T=N/D

Where

T = Takt Time

N = Nett time available (seconds or minutes / day)

D = Demand (customer demand)

Using the formula above; if we have a demand of 300 units per day and a 7.6 hour nett work day (excluding breaks) we would have a takt time of 91.2 seconds.

I have usually calculated the takt time in seconds however there have been instances where minutes have been required due to low customer demand and long cycle times.

Obviously the available time is easy to work out, where many people struggle is calculating the customer demand. Unfortunately many businesses don't understand what their customer demand is let alone calculate the takt time. Whether you have high or low customer demand and whether you have fast or slow cycle times it is important to know your takt time. I often hear "but we have endless demand" or ""we cannot satisfy the demand, so it isn't important; we just need to reduce the cycle time". No, you need a target; even if you use the promised daily delivery quantity. Although this may not satisfy demand it is a quantity agreed by the customer – in this instance it could be labelled as the agreed customer demand and can be used for the calculation of the takt time.

The Three Slips and Kaizen

Standardised work can be implemented effectively without the use of the three slips; I've seen it work a number of times (the book 7 Steps To A Lean Business details how this has been achieved). There are a number of reasons why it is more effective by following the tried and tested use of the three slips. The slips will become the:

- Work instructions
- Audit template
- Quality standards
- OHS procedures
- Benchmarking tools

The three slips are:

- Production Capacity Sheet
- Standardised Work Combination Table
- Standardised Work Chart

The following three chapters will detail how these documents are completed; while they are easily explained in theory we will be following an example through the process. This will make the learning more practical and encourage you to practice these theories in your own organisation as soon as practical to reinforce them and to gain a thorough understanding.

Before we start, we need to look at why we are going through this process with some kaizen theory; more detail can be found in 7 Steps To A Lean Business and Your 60 Minute Lean Business - Kaizen. Roughly translated kaizen means "change for better" this is commonly known as continuous improvement in Western business practices. The objective of continuous improvement is similar to lean business systems:

- The removal of waste from the processes to increase the value add to the customer

This will have a positive impact on customer satisfaction and will also increase profits. If we look at how an organisation can increase profits there are three options:

1. Increase sale price
    a. In most market segments the price is largely governed by the market itself (market driven). Unless you are operating in a niche market or with a niche product/service.
2. Increase sales volume
    a. Once again, this is largely market driven.
    b. Every market has a ceiling. Once reached the prices will drop from saturation.
    c. As the market moves closer to saturation, the marketing costs increase thereby reducing profits further.
3. Reduce operating costs
    a. By reducing operating costs, sales price and sales volume can be maintained and deliver increased profits

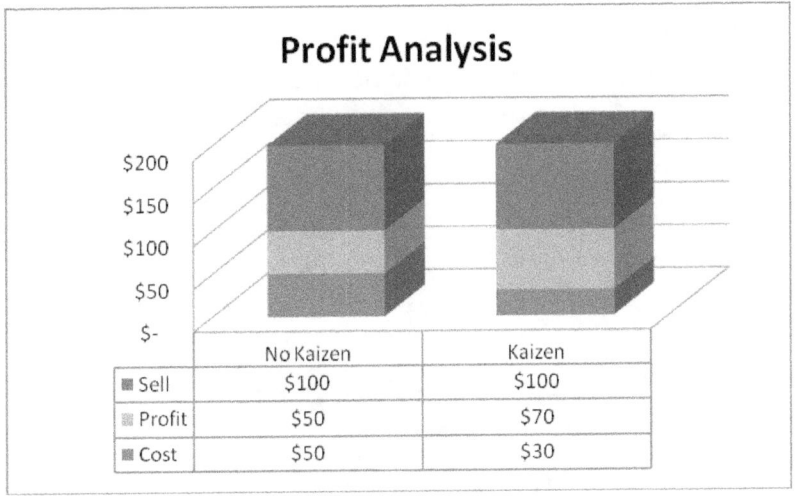

These cost reductions are achieved through elimination and reduction of waste from the processes. The waste can be identified through completing the current state three slips or alternatively through Value Stream Mapping (more on this in an upcoming book).

Let's have a look at how waste can impact the process cycle. The work elements within a process can be divided into three types:
1. Value Add
    a. Work that (from the customers point of view) adds value to the product
2. Non Value Add (Waste)
    a. Work that (from the customers point of view) does not add any value to the product

3. Incidental

   a. Work that must be undertaken to enable the value adding work

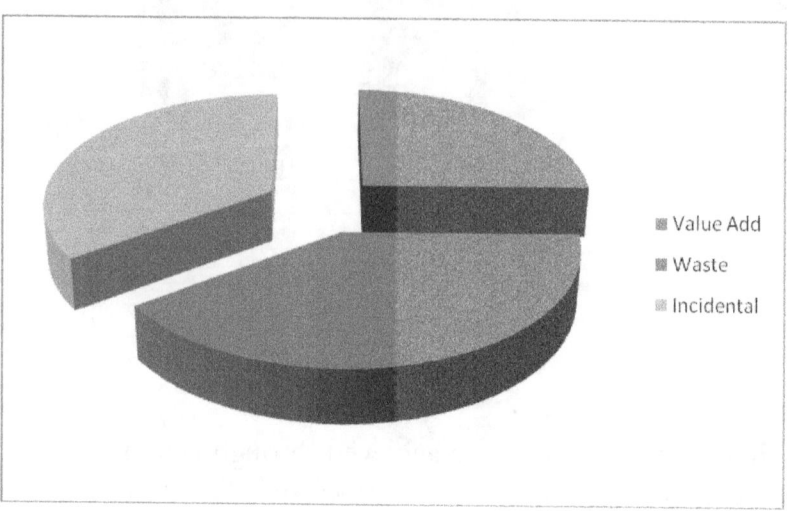

In the above example, 40% of the processing time is lost through waste and only 25% is actually spent adding value. You should notice that the term 'value' is always from the customers point of view; meaning 'what the customer is happy to pay for'. A good example of this is a final cleaning process; is this waste, value add or incidental? Many say this is value add because the customer is happy to pay for a clean product. In reality it is waste though; yes, the customer expects a clean product, however they don't care why it requires cleaning, that is your responsibility as the manufacturer to eliminate the need for the final clean.

The seven wastes of manufacturing are:

1. Waiting
2. Overproduction
3. Reworking
4. Motion
5. Overprocessing
6. Inventory
7. Transportation

Kaizen is how we continuously measure and challenge our processes to improve; standardised work is how we ensure we can consistently deliver this acceptable performance. The documented standardised work process is not necessarily the absolute best process time; it is the best practice for consistently delivering safety, quality and product in accordance with the customer demand. We don't want to produce any less or any more than is required.

Slip 1 – Production Capacity Sheet

Product:		Completed by:				Approved:		Date:
Process Number	Process Name	Machine	Manual Time	Auto Time	Total Time	Change Over	Setup	Capacity	Comments
Total									

Production Capacity Sheet

The production capacity sheet is the first of the three slips. This slip is used to identify the maximum repeatable output from a processing sequence or production line. It is common during training for this sheet not to be used for 100% manual production lines; I disagree, although not every column will be required, this sheet still provides a simple method for calculating your capacity. Follow these steps to successfully complete the sheet.

1. Enter the product number and / or name.
2. Enter the name of the person completing the form. If more than one person is involved in the exercise, all should be added.
3. Leave the approved by cell for now; this will be completed by a supervisor or manager once completed.
4. Enter the date.
5. Enter the process sequence numbers in the far left column.
6. List the process names in the second column.
7. Enter the machine number in the next column. If your machines are not numbered this can be left blank.
8. Enter the manual time – this is the time an operator is performing manual tasks (not waiting).
9. Enter the auto cycle time – this is all time the machine is operating without direct operator input / control.
10. This is usually the manual added to the auto time; an exception to this may be where a portion of the

manual work can be performed while the auto cycle is running.

11. Enter the tool change over frequency in parts. E.g. if the tool requires changing every 100 cycles; enter 100 in the 'Change Over" column.

12. Enter the setup time it takes to perform the tool change in the set up column.

13. Calculate the production capacity for each process sequence. Note: the +1 is for initial setup before the shift starts.

$$\text{Production Capacity} = \frac{\text{Operational time / shift}}{\text{Total Time} + \frac{\text{(Setup Time)}}{\text{(Changeover freq} + 1)}}$$

14. The minimum process capacity down the 'Capacity' column will be the production line capacity.

It isn't unusual to have a great disparity between the maximum and the minimum process capacities. It critically important to plan all production around the lower figure as any planning around the larger figures will be unattainable. This may seem pretty obvious, but I've seen bad planning in this way in many organisations (large multinationals included).

The following diagram shows a completed Production Capacity Sheet. Follow this example through to familiarize yourself with the workings; especially take the time to make sure you fully understand the capacity calculation formula.

Production Capacity Sheet - Training Line

Product:	Training	Completed by:	JT		Approved:			Date:	1/01/2000
Process Number	Process Name	Machine	Manual Time	Auto Time	Total Time	Change Over	Setup	Capacity	Comments
1	One	6	5	35	40	0	0	684	
2	Two	5	6	7	13	200	120	2012	
3	Three	4	4	12	16	0	0	1710	
4	Four	3	5	18	23	1000	60	1186	
5	Five	2	9	42	51	0	0	536	
6	Six	1	3	9	12	0	0	2280	
	Total		32	123	155			536	

In the example above, the overall line capacity is 536 units as process 5 is the limiting element. If you are using a production plan, it is important that this figure be set as the maximum production line capacity.

There are three elements to standardised work:
- Takt Time – as discussed earlier in this book
- Working sequence
    - the optimal sequence of process elements to produce consistent processing time (within takt time) and output quality
    - The work sequence should follow a standard path that reduces the amount of walking between elements
    - The work sequence may be in a forward direction; a reverse direction; or both
- Standard in-process stock
    - the minimum number of work in progress within the process to maintain an efficient flow

How do you quantify the standard in-process stock?

First there are a few guidelines to assist with the examples that will follow: One piece flow is practiced in each of the examples with a single operator following a standard work sequence. For forward only or reverse only the optimum layout would be a U shaped cell to reduce the amount of walking to return to the start.

Situation	In-process stock
Work direction – forward only	0
Work direction – Forward and reverse	1
Manual only cycle	0
Automatic cycle	1

Example 1 – Work direction forward only with manual only machines

When the work sequence only follows a single forward direction there is no added requirement for in-process stock as the work piece can be taken to the next element by the operator.

This method is more suitable for a process made up of manual only machinery. As there is no in-process stock requirement for manual work elements there is zero requirement for in-process stock.

Example 2 – Work direction forward only with automatic machines

Once again there is no requirement for in-process stock, however as this cycle has automatic machines we should have one piece of in-process stock per automatic machine.

As the operator commences the sequence, he will place a part in the first machine

- start the machine and move to the second machine
- remove the already processed part, take the in-process stock and place it in the machine
- start the machine and move to the third machine and so on.
- The operator moves on to the next machine whilst the previous machine is still operating.

If the process includes five automatic machines there is a requirement for four pieces of in-process stock. The first machine does not require in-process stock as raw material is available.

Example 3 – Work direction forwards and reverse with automatic machines

There are some situations where a U shaped cell isn't possible due to constraints. When an inline work cell is in operation there will be considerable waste resulting from walking to return to the starting point.

This waste can be eliminated by introducing a reverse cycle (it's important to note this will only be effective in a work cell consisting of automated machines).

The forward sequence is the same as in example 2, however requires an extra piece of in-process stock (two per machine – one for automatic plus one for reverse sequence). As the operator completes the forward cycle he returns to the last machine

- Removes the processed piece, place the in-process stock in the machine and start the machine

- Move to the second last machine, remove the processed part, place the in-process stock in the machine and start the machine and so forth until he returns to the first machine

- At the first machine he will remove the processed part, insert raw material and start the machine before moving forward to the second machine

Effectively, for each walking cycle of the process line the machines are producing two cycles. This means the walking to return to the start is productive. For a production line consisting of five machines eight pieces of in-process stock will be required.

By following these standard in-process stock principles you will achieve increased productivity with reduced inventory. These principles work effectively for fully manned sequences (reverse cycle will not be required as the operator will not be walking to the start point (no waste). In the situation of a fully manned sequence, one piece of in-process stock will be required per machine for manual or automatic if each element is balanced in time. Line balancing / work load analysis will be further discussed in later in this book.

Slip 2 – Standardised Work Combination Table

The Standardised Work Combination Table (SWCT) is used a tool used for analyzing both manual and automatic work elements against the takt time to determine the best work sequence and load leveling to maintain a cycle time that consistently meets the customer demand (takt time). In essence, SWCT is a mapping tool. Like any mapping tool, the first stage is a capture of the current state followed by analysis before designing the future state.

Before completing the current state SWCT the process needs to be measured. There are a few 'rules' to be followed to give the best results:

- Study an experienced operator to give best results
- The operator must follow a standard (repetitive) process
- Study at least 10 cycles of the process
- Break a large process into smaller studies
- Measure every step. A more detailed study will enable better analysis and lead to more improvements
- Remain out of the way and limit the amount of contact and discussion to before and after the study.
    - o Let the operator know what you are doing and why you are there before the study
    - o Instruct them to follow a repetitive sequence
    - o Wait until after the study to ask questions and gain clarity

Above is a blank example of the Standardised Work Recording Sheet that can be used for the timing study. In

27

the following pages it is further broken down and completed step by step. There is a single example of the Standardised Work Recording Sheet followed by a number of examples of the Standardised Work Combination Charts showing the different approaches to differing processes. The different approaches are almost as many as there are different processes; these cannot all be shown in this book, however the three shown should provide enough to get you going.

1. Manual only process

Dept:	
Process:	
Recorded By:	

Fill in the department, process name and the name of the person performing the study.

Date:	
Operator(s):	
Qty / Shift (Capacity)	

The date of the study, the names of the operators and the process capacity / shift. The takt time, target cycle time and demand / shift.

Takt Time	
Cycle Time (Secs)	
Demand / Shift	

All of the above information, is entered in the header of the sheet and is used to complete the SWCT and / or during the analysis. All of the information should be available if the Capacity Sheet has been completed as in the previous chapter.

Next step is to begin the timing study. Arm yourself with a stopwatch, clipboard and a couple of pencils or pens and begin by discussing with the operators about why you are there, what you are doing and what you require from them.

I tend to start be measuring the overall process 10 times without looking at the individual steps at this stage to give you a baseline for the overall process time. Next I will watch the process for a number of times to make sure I have the element steps clearly defined and recorded on the sheet then making sure the operators are following a repetitive sequence.

The above may seem like waste, however through experience I have learnt this will reduce your rework and improve the quality of your measurements.

Item	Description	1
1	One	5
2	Two	12
3	Three	15
4	Four	23
5	Five	31
6	Six	38
7	Seven	42
8	Eight	49
9	Nine	55
10	Ten	61

In the Description column the process element steps are listed. You will notice the cycle columns are separated into two diagonal cells. At this stage you only enter the aggregate time in the lower or right hand cell. Later the individual times will be added to the upper or left cell. It would be difficult to measure and write the small times without missing the following element.

The following indicates how the individual elements are recorded. As you can see the times are now calculated and entered in the correct cells.

Item	Description	1
1	One	5 / 5
2	Two	7 / 12
3	Three	3 / 15
4	Four	8 / 23
5	Five	8 / 31
6	Six	7 / 38
7	Seven	4 / 42
8	Eight	7 / 49
9	Nine	6 / 55
10	Ten	6 / 61

The process is repeated for at least 5 cycles (for long cycle times) or preferably 10 cycles.

Item	Description	1		2		3		4		5		6		7		8		9		10		Cycle Time	Walk (Secs)
1	One	5	5	6	6	6	6	5	5	7	7	6	5	4	4	5	5	6	5	6	6	5	2
2	Two	7	12	8	14	7	13	7	12	6	13	7	13	9	13	8	13	7	13	7	13	7	3
3	Three	3	15	4	18	3	16	3	15	4	17	3	17	3	16	5	18	3	16	4	17	3	0
4	Four	8	23	9	27	7	23	7	22	8	25	7	24	8	24	9	28	8	24	7	24	7	3
5	Five	8	31	8	35	9	32	8	30	9	34	7	31	8	32	11	39	9	33	8	32	8	3
6	Six	7	38	8	43	8	40	9	39	8	42	9	39	8	40	9	38	8	41	8	40	4	2
7	Seven	4	42	5	48	5	45	6	45	5	47	4	43	5	45	6	44	6	47	5	45	5	0
8	Eight	7	49	6	54	7	52	8	53	6	53	7	50	7	52	8	52	6	53	7	52	6	0
9	Nine	6	55	7	61	7	59	8	61	7	60	7	57	8	60	7	59	8	61	7	59	7	3
10	Ten	6	61	7	68	8	67	5	66	7	67	7	64	6	66	7	66	8	69	5	65	6	0

Above is a snapshot of the completed example. Notice the cycle time column. The lowest repeatable time is entered into this column; not the average time. Using the average time is likely to make your cycle time greater than it needs to be. Using the lowest recorded time will leave you with a cycle time that is not repeatable. Remember, this will become your standard and should be the best repeatable time.

Just as with every other skill with practice you will become better at identifying the elements to be measured and the act of measurement itself. To become a good practitioner these skills need to be practiced across a variety of process types and cycle times.

Now we have the measurement of the elements it's time to introduce the Standardised Work Combination Table. We'll use the measured examples above to maintain a consistent approach and relevance. We have everything in the above sheets we need with the exception of the takt time. For this example we will use a customer demand of 400 units per day. Working on a 7.6hr work day this gives us a takt time of 68.4 seconds. One unit needs to be completed every 68.4 seconds. I'll reiterate here how common it is for organisations to not know this info about their demand; what chance do you have to meet the demand if you don't know what it means!

The following illustration shows a completed SWCT example; note the line at 68 seconds (TT), this is the takt time. The following illustrations will break down how to complete the SWCT for a manual process. You will note the cycle time runs past the takt time by just under 9 seconds; this is an obvious problem that can be seen without needing to have a good understanding of the process or even the documentation – this is the beauty of visual management.

33

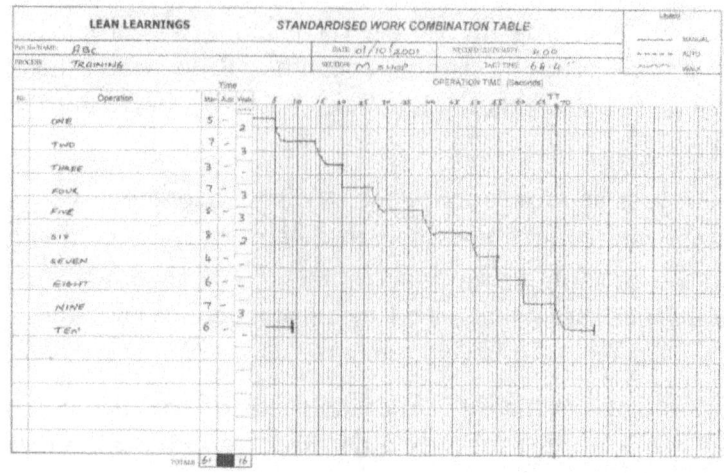

We will now look at the SWCT in more detail in the following illustrations.

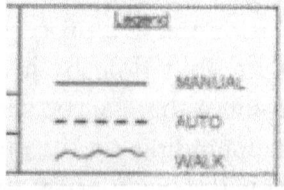

Enter the Part, Process, Date, Section, Number needed per shift and the takt time into the respective cells. Below is the legend for the symbols

List all of the operations in the left column followed by the Manual, Auto (if applicable) and Walking between operations (if applicable).

Operation	Man	Auto	Walk
ONE	5	-	2
TWO	7	-	3
THREE	3	-	-
FOUR	7	-	3
FIVE	5	-	3
SIX	8	-	2
SEVEN	4	-	-
EIGHT	6	-	-
NINE	7	-	3
TEN	6	-	-

Label the horizontal axis of the chart at the major intersections (the example is labelled in five second intervals – this may need to be greater or lesser intervals depending on your takt and cycle time. Draw a vertical red line to indicate the takt time in the relevant position. Next we map the data onto the chart area.

- First draw the manual time for the first operation with a straight continuous line.
- In this example there is no automated operation – this will be shown in the second example
- Next drop to the next operation

- Count the walking time between operations one and two and mark the start of the next manual operation before drawing the manual time for the second operation. Continue this for each operation until either finished or until the takt time line is reached.

The diagram below illustrates the straight lines for the manual time. Notice the squiggle line between the manual times, these lines indicates the walking time. Between operations three and four below there is no walking time; this is indicated with a straight vertical line.

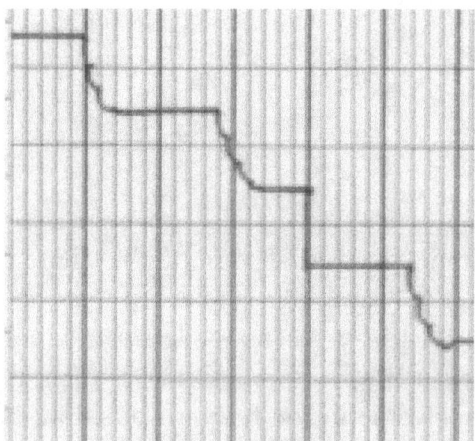

This is all pretty simple,, but what happens when we get to the takt time line? The idea of standardised work is to produce what the customer wants; no more, no less. So if the cycle time is less than the takt time, this is waste. The operator will have two choices, stop and rest, or overproduce. Neither of these two options are ok. Another possibility is the cycle time is greater than the takt time; this will result in the production target not being met. The diagram below indicates how we draw the latter.

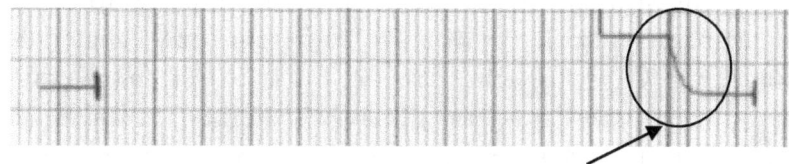

Notice the takt time line (see arrow), the last operation in this example continues past the line. In this situation, the line is continued past the takt time line, however is also drawn from the left side – also note the line from the left starting from three seconds. This is because the preceding operation completed at the takt time; the three seconds is the walk time between operations. Further operations would be drawn from the end of the operation on the left – only the initial operation to continue past the takt time is drawn past the takt time line.

We'll discuss how we will use this information in the last two chapters. For now we will look at the second example which includes automated cycle times.

2. Manual and Auto Process

For a process with manual and auto times you will need to complete two timing study work sheets. The first will be for the manual process and the second will be for the auto time. In most instances, the auto time will be very stable as there are limited variables; this is not always the case though, there can be circumstances where material variability can affect the auto cycle times. When the auto cycle times are not stable the sample size will need to be similar to that of the manual time; in some extreme situations it may be necessary to put in place multiple standardised work times for different raw materials standards. Obviously the first option is to set engineering and quality standards for the raw materials, however in some industries this can be difficult due to seasonal changes (fresh foods in particular) and issues of raw materials availability. I have worked on processes where the only answer was to adjust the operating settings to cater for changes in the raw materials – some things are just out of your control unfortunately.

For this exercise we will assume we have a stable auto process to eliminate the need to go through the measurement scenario. Below is a short explanation of the process to be mapped.

Process:
This process includes a robot to perform the auto cycle. The robot is manually started and has a carousel to enable unloading and loading while in operation. Unless there has been significant maintenance performed, the shift will always commence with the machine leaded and ready for operation meaning the cycle will start with the auto cycle.

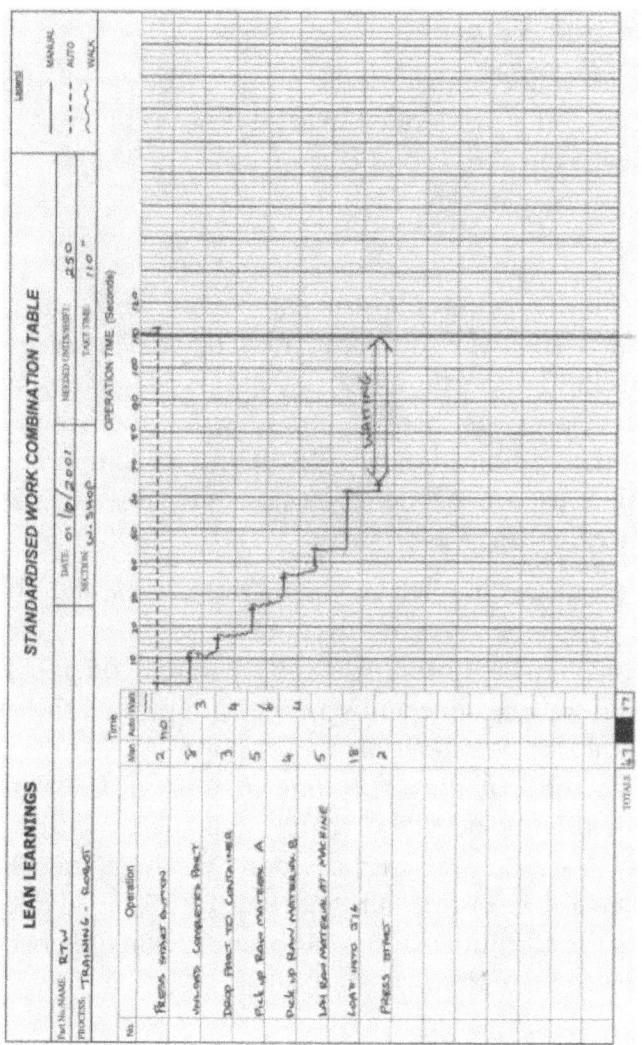

In the above example you can see the auto cycle time runs for the entire takt time, however the manual time is less than the takt time and is shown as waiting time.

3. Auto Inline Process

An inline auto process needs to be handled a little differently. There is limited manual time and increased auto time. Just as in the second example the line will always start with in process stock at each station.

Process:

This process consists of 6 machines all closely positioned and with different auto machining times. The auto machine time runs just under the takt time, however even if it ran over the takt time it would be irrelevant; as long as the combination of manual and walking time is less than or equal to the takt time you are able to meet the customer demand.

In this example a single operator is running the line. If the customer demand was increased dramatically an option would be to increase the operators on the line to reduce to walking time and synchronize some of the manual cycle time. You will see in the example (next page) more than one third of the cycle time (manual + walking) is in walking; this includes the return walk to the start of the process. You can see that the auto machine time has no relevance as long as the auto machine of no single operation exceeds the takt time. If this did occur it would be necessary to engineer a solution.

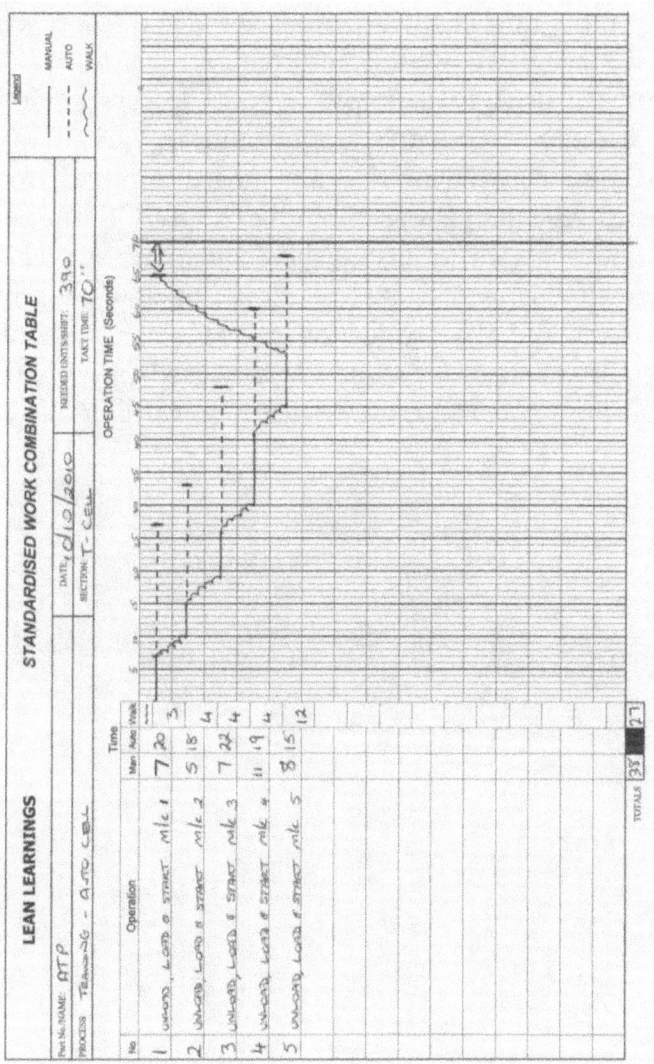

The variations to the SWCT are almost endless as each different situation needs to be recorded in a slightly different manner. Once you have used these tools enough you will be able to determine the best recording method.

In the final chapter "Standardised Work and Kaizen" we will discuss how the information identified in this chapter can be used to improve your processes. However even without identifying opportunities, what has been achieved so far will provide a standard approach to your processes with standard outcomes. The SWCT can be used as an auditing tool to ensure these operating standards are maintained. Planned delivery targets can now be achieved consistently and the production planners can be confident the requirements will be met. When used on conjunction with quality standards, the SWCT is a powerful tool.

Slip 3 – Standardised Work Chart

The third and final slip is the Standardised Work Chart (SWC), this compliments the first two slips by providing a visual display of the layout and workflow. This display includes in-process stock, safety stations and quality inspection stations.

Any new employee or observer (management, supplier, customer etc) can easily understand how the process flows, where the process starts and finishes and how much in-process stock is required to run the process. This document provides:

- Training documentation
- Audit tool for supervisors, quality officers etc.
- Tool for management (onsite or visiting) to quickly understand process
- Quick and easy lookup reminder for operators
- Easy check of in-process stock requirements
- Identified safety and quality inspection stations
- Forms a part of your visual management system

The following example follows the first example from the previous two chapters to maintain consistency. The work-cell is a U shaped cell and it can be clearly seen where the process starts, finishes and the direction of flow.

You will notice the left side of the slip is quite similar to the Standardised Work Combination Table.

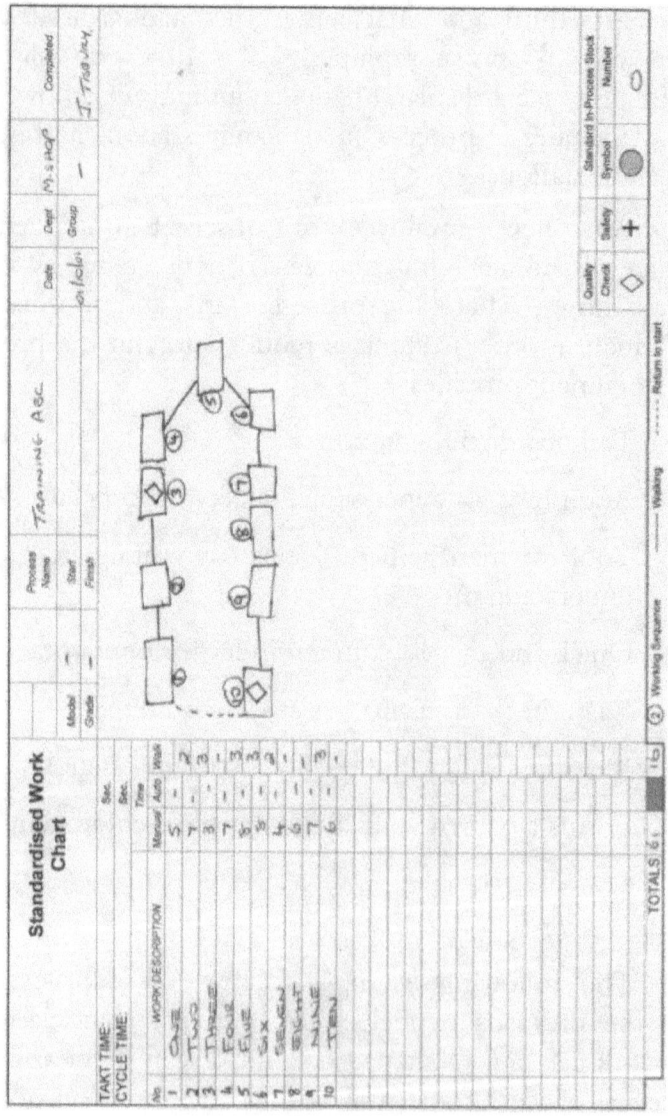

Follow the below steps to develop the SWC:

- The header area can be filled from information gathered and recorded on previous documents
- This information such as Takt Time, Total Cycle Time etc are recorded on multiple documents to enable the viewer to be sure all of the documents are of the same revision
- Fill in the operation name in the Work Description column
- Enter the manual, auto cycle times and the walk time in the relevant columns
- Record the in-process stock in the lower right hand cell

Now for the drawing; the process or cell layout is drawn in the large canvas area. Draw the layout in its current state as close to scale as possible without spending excessive time. The order of the following steps is not critical, however this is the order that I generally follow.

Next task is to number the work stations in order of the process steps. It is not uncommon for work stations to be used for multiple process steps. Next a continuous line is drawn to join the process steps; arrows are not necessary as the process numbers indicate the direction without leaving the canvas too cluttered. Finally the quality inspection points, safety stations and in-process stock are drawn onto the relevant work stations.

When combined with the previous sheets we now have a process that is documented against the following criteria:

- Takt Time
- Demand
- Capacity
- Cycle Time
- Processing time
    - Manual
    - Auto (Machine)
    - Walking (Transport)
- Process flow
- In-process stock
- Quality inspection points
- Safety stations

This documentation can be used for training, auditing, process review and visitor / management awareness.

Other Documents

In addition to the three slips, other documentation are useful in any analysis or improvement activities. The following documents are not an exhaustive list however will provide a starting point.

Work Load Chart

The work load chart (also called a Yamazumi Chart) is used to visualize and analyze work loads at different workstations or operators within a process. It is a very useful tool used to determine overburden / under utilization and provides another way of looking at problems meeting demand. The work load chart can be measured against takt time or cycle time and can be used for any process with more than two elements to support the previous documents.

Work load charts are useful for analyzing elements within a process, processes within a production line; can be used for manufacturing or business processes and can even be used to analyze elements across the value stream combining business processes and manufacturing / supply chain processes.

Below is an example of a relatively well balanced process. The cycle time is one second less than the takt time and there is a three second difference between the shortest and longest element times. This work load could be balanced slightly more evenly, however the benefits

47

would not be significant enough to warrant too much time or money to be invested.

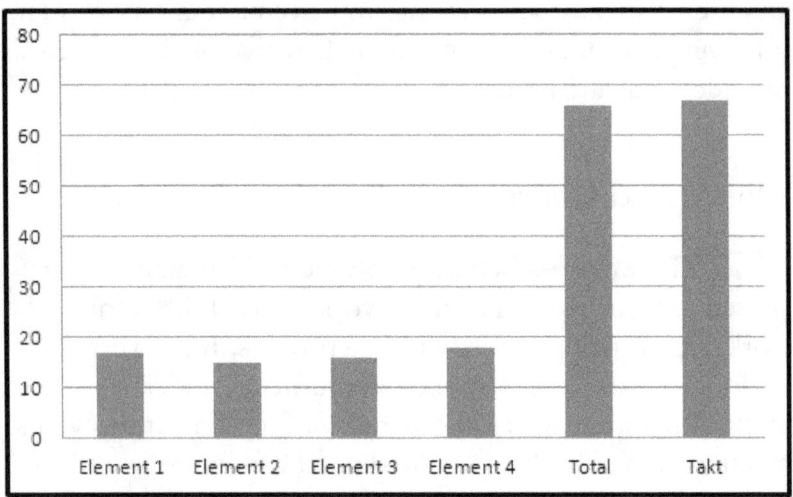

The next example is a little more challenging, the cycle time and takt times are the same as the first example however the work load is quite unbalanced. Note there is 13 seconds difference between the shortest and longest element times. Depending on the type of work, machine / manual work ratio, OHS exposure and duration of exposure this example may warrant further analysis and efforts to improve the balance.

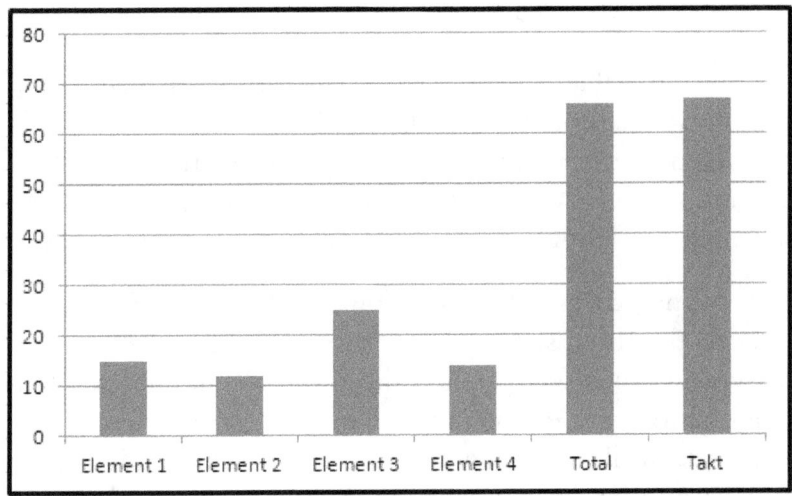

In situations where the cycle time is greater than the takt time there are obviously more challenges to overcome. In these instances it is necessary to analyse the process with the Standardised Work Combination Table to identify where the process can be improved.

Value Stream Map

The Value Stream Map (VSM) is often seen as an alternative method of Standardised Work, and while this can be an alternative, it can also supplement the three slips method. There will be a future book in this series to specifically discuss VSM so the detail here will be minimal.

The process of developing a VSM is similar in many ways to the three slips, in fact the information collected in the earlier steps will provide the most of the information required to complete the VSM. The real purpose of a VSM is to clearly illustrate and measure the value adding and more importantly, the non-value adding work elements within a process. With these elements identified you can then determine how to best eliminate or reduce the non-value adding time (waste). This comes back to the heart of lean methodology.

The below diagram is a simple current state VSM.

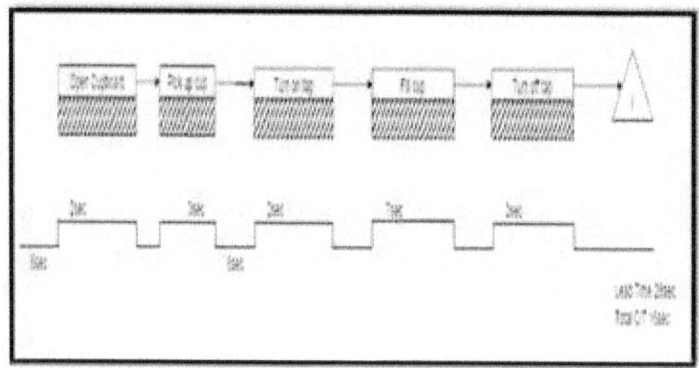

The process steps (elements) are along the top with the far right triangle signifying inventory. Along the bottom is the timeline; the raised sections indicate value adding time; the lower sections indicate non-value adding time. This diagram enables easy identification of both the non-value adding elements and the time (waste) created by these elements. The far lower right indicates the total cycle time (raised) and the total non-value adding time (lower). A detailed approach to developing a VSM will be in the upcoming book 'Your 60 Minute Lean Business – VSM.'

Quality Standards

A lean system is far more than just performing the tasks in a timely manner. For true efficiency to be achieved it is important to touch on the role quality plays in achieving standardised work. The term 'standardised work' means to realise consistent outputs in regards to meeting demand (time), quality and cost. Having clearly defined quality standards plays an important part in achieving this consistency.

So what are quality standards? It is common to think of written standards such as QS9000, ISO9001, TS16949 when discussing quality standards, however we are talking about standards at a more process management level. What we are talking about is clearly defining the output expectations; actual specifications, tolerances, upper and lower limits etc. When the standards are set it is possible to monitor performance against the standards and make corrections or adjustments to the process.

Without first setting these standards it is very difficult to measure the output quality of the process. Just as it is important to monitor the process time against takt time, it is critical to monitor the quality performance against the standards or specifications. The monitoring frequency should depend on how well controlled the process is. With a new process, the frequency should be higher until consistency is achieved. Once consistency is achieved, the frequency can be reduced; monitoring should not stop. In the instance of a defect being identified the frequency should be increased again until the process is back in control. There are formulas available for process control and are will be discussed in the future book "Your 60 Minute Lean Business – Jidoka".

For greater effect, the quality standards should be displayed visually at the work area at every processing step. The earlier in the process a defect is identified, the less the cost of poor quality; both in materials and labour. Poor quality also has an obvious negative impact on the performance against takt time.

With the quality standards documented, we now have the three slips and the quality standards all displayed at each process.

Analysis and Kaizen

Measuring the current state by itself is not going to improve anything. Only through analysis and kaizen or continuous improvement will any real benefit be achieved. After the measurement is complete there are a number of common waste types that can be identified through the three slips. The seven wastes are:

- Waiting
- Overproduction
- Rework
- Motion
- Processing (excess)
- Inventory
- Transport

Analyze the processes against the above criteria and eliminate or reduce the amount and impact of those wastes that are present. The biggest waste of the above list in overproduction; this is because overproduction will often result in the other types of wastes occurring. For example, overproduction will lead to inventory, which will lead to transport. If the inventory sits for any length of time it can result in cleaning (excess processing) or rework should the design or specifications change between production runs.

There are a number of ways to reduce the waste including:

- Re-engineering of the process

- Cell layout to reduce motion
- Improve quality to reduce rework
- Improved production planning to reduce inventory
- Implementation of pull systems to eliminate inventory
- Process alignment to reduce or eliminate waiting
- Elimination of non-value adding operations
- Improved plant layout to reduce transportation

There will be times when a single change can provide significant improvement, however as your processes become more mature you will need a combination of fixes to achieve the improvements required.

Next Steps

Standardised work by itself will provide benefits, however these benefits will be limited if used in isolation without other lean business tools. Many businesses do not require all of the available tools; it is a good practice to become familiar with all of the tools to enable you to choose the right tools for each problem encountered.

Going through this for the first time is only the beginning. Ownership of the slips and process must be with the teams; with strong leadership, the teams can develop the processes through continuous improvement. Do not forget the seven wastes – WORMPIT. Waiting, Overproduction, Rework, Motion, Processing, Inventory and Transportation.

Don't fall into the trap of improving the process time to be less than the takt time and overproducing (inventory). This is a common over correction. Remember to stop production once the required quantity has been produced.

Many small improvements sustained and built upon will also result in your organisation achieving far more than improved processes; you will develop a kaizen mindset in your employees which will lead to sustained growth.

www.ingramcontent.com/pod-product-compliance
Lightning Source LLC
Chambersburg PA
CBHW061519180526
45171CB00001B/245